This book belongs to :

©**Sigal Adler**

No part of this publication may be reproduced, photocopied, translated, stored in a database or Distributing any form or by any means (electronic, optical or mechanical, including photocopying or recording) without prior written permission of the author.

Publish and printed in USA, 2017

You're Not My Monster

By Sigal Adler

When little Dan started to sleep on his own

His parents were proud of how much he'd grown

They gave him a monster, a sweet little doll

To prove to the world – he was not scared at all!

Their first night together was quite a change

Dan's little monster looked pretty strange

But Dan loved him still and held him so tight

To prove he was not scared at all in the night.

The second night, too, without even a peep

The two brand-new friends got ready to sleep

Dan fell asleep without stopping to think,

But woke up much later to go get a drink.

But when Dan then returned to his room

A surprise waited there, deep in the gloom

His monster was gone, something wasn't right

Instead, a big monster stood there in his sight.

The big monster winked: "Hello little boy!

How was your day? What's your favorite toy?

This may sound odd the first time we meet,

But tell me, what is there around here to eat?"

Now Dan was quite shocked at what he had found,

A big hungry monster, tossing rinds on the ground.

"You're not my monster!" Dan shouted at last.

Oh, dear," said the creature, "And please, not so fast…"

The creature said that everyone knew

That one BIGGER monster was better than two!

"So I swallowed your monster so I could grow

But I'll give it back – if you only say so."

The monster jiggled and wiggled about

Trying to get Dan's monster back out.

There were TWO monsters now over there by the bed

But neither was Dan's – and the newer one said,

"I swallowed your monster, I just didn't know,

But I'll give it back – if you only say so."

And with a great effort, she huffed and she puffed

Out popped a monster much smaller and fluffed.

The room was so crowded, all three in a pack,

But poor Dan just wanted his own monster back.

The new monster was a most grumpy one,
He tried and he tried, though it wasn't much fun,
And finally out popped another – one more!
Squashed into the room, with no space on the floor.

The newest monster to arrive

Was midnight monster number five.

Dan at last could take no more:

"I want my monster from before!"

He tried to move but found no space

No room to breathe, no empty place

Watermelon rinds tossed low and high

And sleepy Dan was about to cry.

The smallest monster said, "Don't worry,

"We'll get your monster in a hurry."

She huffed and puffed and turned bright red –

And Dan's monster popped out on the bed!

Well, Dan loved his monster most of all

Not minding at a bit that it was so small

His parents had chosen it with love and care

And he knew a monster this special was rare.

Dan was exhausted by all the night brought

But now what? He just stood there and thought.

There were monsters around, eating so loud,

So how could he fall asleep in this crowd?

He asked very nicely, "Hey guys, are you done?"

"Sure!" they agreed. "And we've had so much fun!"

Dan woke up amazed at the dream he'd had there…

But why were there watermelon rinds everywhere???

Adler.sigal@gmail.com

CPSIA information can be obtained
at www.ICGtesting.com
Printed in the USA
LVHW070026270420
654478LV00009B/28